TENEBRAE

TENEBRAE

Geoffrey Hill

Boston

HOUGHTON MIFFLIN COMPANY   1979

First American Edition 1979

Library of Congress Cataloging in Publication Data

Hill, Geoffrey.
  Tenebrae.
  I. Title.
PR6015.I4735T4 1979   821'.9'14   78-26005
ISBN 0-395-27610-1

Printed in the United States of America

P 10 9 8 7 6 5 4 3 2 1

CONTENTS

This is a very ancient land indeed;
Aiaia formerly or Cythera
Or Celidon the hollow forest called;
This is the country Ulysses and Hermod
Entered afraid; by ageing poets sought . . .

THE PENTECOST CASTLE

It is terrible to desire and not
possess, and terrible to possess
and not desire.

W. B. YEATS

What we love in other human
beings is the hoped-for satisfaction
of our desire. We do not love their
desire. If what we loved in them
was their desire, then we should
love them as ourself.

SIMONE WEIL

1

They slew by night
upon the road
Medina's pride
Olmedo's flower

shadows warned him
not to go
not to go
along that road

weep for your lord
Medina's pride
Olmedo's flower
there in the road

2

Down in the orchard
I met my death
under the briar rose
I lie slain

I was going
to gather flowers
my love waited
among the trees

down in the orchard
I met my death
under the briar rose
I lie slain

3

You watchers on the wall
grown old with care
I too looked from the wall
I shall look no more

tell us what you saw
the lord I sought to serve
caught in the thorn grove
his blood on his brow

you keepers of the wall
what friend or enemy
sets free the cry
of the bell

4

At dawn the Mass
burgeons from stone
a Jesse tree
of resurrection

budding with candle
flames the gold
and the white wafers
of the feast

and ghosts for love
void a few tears
of wax upon
forlorn altars

5

Goldfinch and hawk
and the grey aspen tree
I have run to the river
mother call me home

the leaves glint in the wind
turning their quiet song
the wings flash and are still
I sleep in the shade

when I cried out you
made no reply
tonight I shall pass by
without a sound

6

Slowly my heron flies
pierced by the blade
mounting in slow pain
strikes the air with its cries

goes seeking the high rocks
where no man can climb
where the wild balsam stirs
by the little stream

the rocks the high rocks
are brimming with flowers
there love grows and there love
rests and is saved

7

I went out early
to the far field
ermine and lily
and yet a child

Love stood before me
in that place
prayers could not lure me
to Christ's house

Christ the deceiver
took all I had
his darkness ever
my fair reward

8

And you my spent heart's treasure
my yet unspent desire
measurer past all measure
cold paradox of fire

as seeker so forsaken
consentingly denied
your solitude a token
the sentries at your side

fulfilment to my sorrow
indulgence of your prey
the sparrowhawk the sparrow
the nothing that you say

9

This love will see me dead
he has the place in mind
where I am free to die
be true at last true love

my love meet me half-way
I bear no sword of fear
where you dwell I
dwell also says my lord

dealing his five wounds
so cunning and so true
of love to rouse this death
I die to sleep in love

10

St James and St John
bless the road she has gone
St John and St James
a rosary of names

child-beads of fingered bread
never-depleted heart's food
the nominal the real
subsistence past recall

bread we shall never break
love-runes we cannot speak
scrolled effigy of a cry
our passion its display

11

If the night is dark
and the way short
why do you hold back
dearest heart

though I may never
see you again
touch me I will shiver
at the unseen

the night is so dark
the way so short
why do you not break
o my heart

12

Married and not for love
you of all women
you of all women
my soul's darling my love

faithful to my desire
lost in the dream's grasp where
shall I find you everywhere
unmatched in my desire

each of us dispossessed
so richly in my sleep
I rise out of my sleep
crying like one possessed

13

Splendidly-shining darkness
proud citadel of meekness
likening us our unlikeness
majesty of our distress

emptiness ever thronging
untenable belonging
how long until this longing
end in unending song

and soul for soul discover
no strangeness to dissever
and lover keep with lover
a moment and for ever

14

As he is wounded
I am hurt
he bleeds from pride
I from my heart

as he is dying
I shall live
in grief desiring
still to grieve

as he is living
I shall die
sick of forgiving
such honesty

15

I shall go down
to the lovers' well
and wash this wound
that will not heal

beloved soul
what shall you see
nothing at all
yet eye to eye

depths of non-being
perhaps too clear
my desire dying
as I desire

LACHRIMAE

or

Seven tears figured in seven passionate Pavans

Passions I allow, and loves I approve, onely
I would wish that men would alter their
object and better their intent.

ST ROBERT SOUTHWELL, *Mary Magdalen's
Funeral Tears*, 1591.

1. Lachrimae Verae

Crucified Lord, you swim upon your cross
and never move. Sometimes in dreams of hell
the body moves but moves to no avail
and is at one with that eternal loss.

You are the castaway of drowned remorse,
you are the world's atonement on the hill.
This is your body twisted by our skill
into a patience proper for redress.

I cannot turn aside from what I do;
you cannot turn away from what I am.
You do not dwell in me nor I in you

however much I pander to your name
or answer to your lords of revenue,
surrendering the joys that they condemn.

2. The Masque of Blackness

Splendour of life so splendidly contained,
brilliance made bearable. It is the east
light's embodiment, fit to be caressed,
the god Amor with his eyes of diamond,

celestial worldliness on which has dawned
intelligence of angels, Midas' feast,
the stony hunger of the dispossessed
locked into Eden by their own demand.

Self-love, the slavish master of this trade,
conquistador of fashion and remark,
models new heavens in his masquerade,

its images intense with starry work,
until he tires and all that he has made
vanishes in the chaos of the dark.

3. Martyrium

The Jesus-faced man walking crowned with flies
who swats the roadside grass or glances up
at the streaked gibbet with its birds that swoop,
who scans his breviary while the sweat dries,

fades, now, among the fading tapestries,
brooches of crimson tears where no eyes weep,
a mouth unstitched into a rimless cup,
torn clouds the cauldrons of the martyrs' cries.

Clamorous love, its faint and baffled shout,
its grief that would betray him to our fear,
he suffers for our sake, or does not hear

above the hiss of shadows on the wheat.
Viaticum transfigures earth's desire
in rising vernicles of summer air.

4. Lachrimae Coactae

Crucified Lord, however much I burn
to be enamoured of your paradise,
knowing what ceases and what will not cease,
frightened of hell, not knowing where to turn,

I fall between harsh grace and hurtful scorn.
You are the crucified who crucifies,
self-withdrawn even from your own device,
your trim-plugged body, wreath of rakish thorn.

What grips me then, or what does my soul grasp?
If I grasp nothing what is there to break?
You are beyond me, innermost true light,

uttermost exile for no exile's sake,
king of our earth not caring to unclasp
its void embrace, the semblance of your quiet.

5. Pavana Dolorosa

Loves I allow and passions I approve:
Ash-Wednesday feasts, ascetic opulence,
the wincing lute, so real in its pretence,
itself a passion amorous of love.

Self-wounding martyrdom, what joys you have,
true-torn among this fictive consonance,
music's creation of the moveless dance,
the decreation to which all must move.

Self-seeking hunter of forms, there is no end
to such pursuits. None can revoke your cry.
Your silence is an ecstasy of sound

and your nocturnals blaze upon the day.
I founder in desire for things unfound.
I stay amid the things that will not stay.

6. Lachrimae Antiquae Novae

Crucified Lord, so naked to the world,
you live unseen within that nakedness,
consigned by proxy to the judas-kiss
of our devotion, bowed beneath the gold,

with re-enactments, penances foretold:
scentings of love across a wilderness
of retrospection, wild and objectless
longings incarnate in the carnal child.

Beautiful for themselves the icons fade;
the lions and the hermits disappear.
Triumphalism feasts on empty dread,

fulfilling triumphs of the festal year.
We find you wounded by the token spear.
Dominion is swallowed with your blood.

7. Lachrimae Amantis

What is there in my heart that you should sue
so fiercely for its love? What kind of care
brings you as though a stranger to my door
through the long night and in the icy dew

seeking the heart that will not harbour you,
that keeps itself religiously secure?
At this dark solstice filled with frost and fire
your passion's ancient wounds must bleed anew.

So many nights the angel of my house
has fed such urgent comfort through a dream,
whispered 'your lord is coming, he is close'

that I have drowsed half-faithful for a time
bathed in pure tones of promise and remorse:
'tomorrow I shall wake to welcome him.'

AN APOLOGY FOR THE REVIVAL OF CHRISTIAN ARCHITECTURE IN ENGLAND

the spiritual, Platonic old England . . .
STC, *Anima Poetae*

'Your situation', said Coningsby, looking up
the green and silent valley, 'is absolutely
poetic.'
'I try sometimes to fancy', said Mr Millbank,
with a rather fierce smile, 'that I am in the
New World.'
BENJAMIN DISRAELI, *Coningsby*

1. Quaint Mazes

And, after all, it is to them we return.
Their triumph is to rise and be our hosts:
lords of unquiet or of quiet sojourn,
those muddy-hued and midge-tormented ghosts.

On blustery lilac-bush and terrace-urn
bedaubed with bloom Linnaean pentecosts
put their pronged light; the chilly fountains burn.
Religion of the heart, with trysts and quests

and pangs of consolation, its hawk's hood
twitched off for sweet carnality, again
rejoices in old hymns of servitude,

haunting the sacred well, the hidden shrine.
It is the ravage of the heron wood;
it is the rood blazing upon the green.

2. Damon's Lament for his Clorinda, Yorkshire 1654

November rips gold foil from the oak ridges.
Dour folk huddle in High Hoyland, Penistone.
The tributaries of the Sheaf and Don
bulge their dull spate, cramming the poor bridges.

The North Sea batters our shepherds' cottages
from sixty miles. No sooner has the sun
swung clear above earth's rim than it is gone.
We live like gleaners of its vestiges

knowing we flourish, though each year a child
with the set face of a tomb-weeper is put down
for ever and ever. Why does the air grow cold

in the region of mirrors? And who is this clown
doffing his mask at the masked threshold
to selfless raptures that are all his own?

3. Who are these coming to the Sacrifice?

High voices in domestic chapels; praise;
praise-worthy feuds; new-burgeoned spires that
    sprung
crisp-leaved as though from dropping-wells. The
    young
ferns root among our vitrified tears.

What an elopement that was: the hired chaise
tore through the fir-grove, scattered kinsmen flung
buckshot and bridles, and the tocsin swung
from the tarred bellcote dappled with dove-smears.

Wires tarnish in gilt corridors, in each room
stiff with the bric-a-brac of loss and gain.
Love fled, truly outwitted, through a swirl

of long-laid dust. Today you sip and smile
though still not quite yourself. Guarding its pane
the spider looms against another storm.

4. A Short History of British India (I)

Make miniatures of the once-monstrous theme:
the red-coat devotees, mêlées of wheels,
Jagannath's lovers. With indifferent aim
unleash the rutting cannon at the walls

of forts and palaces; pollute the wells.
Impound the memoirs for their bankrupt shame,
fantasies of true destiny that kills
'under the sanction of the English name'.

Be moved by faith, obedience without fault,
the flawless hubris of heroic guilt,
the grace of visitation; and be stirred

by all her god-quests, her idolatries,
in conclave of abiding injuries,
sated upon the stillness of the bride.

5. A Short History of British India (II)

Suppose they sweltered here three thousand years
patient for our destruction. There is a greeting
beyond the act. Destiny is the great thing,
true lord of annexation and arrears.

Our law-books overrule the emperors.
The mango is the bride-bed of light. Spring
jostles the flame-tree. But new mandates bring
new images of faith, good subahdars!

The flittering candles of the wayside shrines
melt into dawn. The sun surmounts the dust.
Krishna from Radha lovingly untwines.

Lugging the earth, the oxen bow their heads.
The alien conscience of our days is lost
among the ruins and on endless roads.

6. A Short History of British India (III)

Malcolm and Frere, Colebrooke and Elphinstone,
the life of empire like the life of the mind
'simple, sensuous, passionate', attuned
to the clear theme of justice and order, gone.

Gone the ascetic pastimes, the Persian
scholarship, the wild boar run to ground,
the watercolours of the sun and wind.
Names rise like outcrops on the rich terrain,

like carapaces of the Mughal tombs
lop-sided in the rice-fields, boarded-up
near railway-sidings and small aerodromes.

'India's a peacock-shrine next to a shop
selling mangola, sitars, lucky charms,
heavenly Buddhas smiling in their sleep.'

7. Loss and Gain

Pitched high above the shallows of the sea
lone bells in gritty belfries do not ring
but coil a far and inward echoing
out of the air that thrums. Enduringly,

fuchsia-hedges fend between cliff and sky;
brown stumps of headstones tamp into the ling
the ruined and the ruinously strong.
Platonic England grasps its tenantry

where wild-eyed poppies raddle tawny farms
and wild swans root in lily-clouded lakes.
Vulnerable to each other the twin forms

of sleep and waking touch the man who wakes
to sudden light, who thinks that this becalms
even the phantoms of untold mistakes.

8. Vocations

While friends defected, you stayed and were sure,
fervent in reason, watchful of each name:
a signet-seal's unostentatious gem
gleams against walnut on the escritoire,

focus of reckoning and judicious prayer.
This is the durable covenant, a room
quietly furnished with stuff of martyrdom,
lit by the flowers and moths from your own shire,

by silvery vistas frothed with convolvulus –
radiance of dreams hardly to be denied.
The twittering pipistrelle, so strange and close,

plucks its curt flight through the moist eventide;
the children thread among old avenues
of snowberries, clear-calling as they fade.

9. The Laurel Axe

Autumn resumes the land, ruffles the woods
with smoky wings, entangles them. Trees shine
out from their leaves, rocks mildew to moss-green;
the avenues are spread with brittle floods.

Platonic England, house of solitudes,
rests in its laurels and its injured stone,
replete with complex fortunes that are gone,
beset by dynasties of moods and clouds.

It stands, as though at ease with its own world,
the mannerly extortions, languid praise,
all that devotion long since bought and sold,

the rooms of cedar and soft-thudding baize,
tremulous boudoirs where the crystals kissed
in cabinets of amethyst and frost.

10. Fidelities

Remember how, at seven years, the decrees
were brought home: child-soul must register
for Christ's dole, be allotted its first Easter,
blanch-white and empty, chilled by the lilies,

betrothed among the well-wishers and spies.
Reverend Mother, breakfastless, could feast her
constraint on terracotta and alabaster
and brimstone and the sweets of paradise.

Theology makes good bedside reading. Some
who are lost covet scholastic proof,
subsistence of probation, modest balm.

The wooden wings of justice borne aloof,
we close our eyes to Anselm and lie calm.
All night the cisterns whisper in the roof.

11. Idylls of the King

The pigeon purrs in the wood; the wood has gone;
dark leaves that flick to silver in the gust,
and the marsh-orchids and the heron's nest,
goldgrimy shafts and pillars of the sun.

Weightless magnificence upholds the past.
Cement recesses smell of fur and bone
and berries wrinkle in the badger-run
and wiry heath-fern scatters its fresh rust.

'O clap your hands' so that the dove takes flight,
bursts through the leaves with an untidy sound,
plunges its wings into the green twilight

above this long-sought and forsaken ground,
the half-built ruins of the new estate,
warheads of mushrooms round the filter-pond.

12. The Eve of St Mark

Stroke the small silk with your whispering hands,
godmother; nod and nod from the half-gloom;
broochlight intermittent between the fronds,
the owl immortal in its crystal dome.

Along the mantelpiece veined lustres trill,
the clock discounts us with a telling chime.
Familiar ministrants, clerks-of-appeal,
burnish upon the threshold of the dream:

churchwardens in wing-collars bearing scrolls
of copyhold well-tinctured and well-tied.
Your photo-albums loved by the boy-king

preserve in sepia waterglass the souls
of distant cousins, virgin till they died,
and the lost delicate suitors who could sing.

13. The Herefordshire Carol

So to celebrate that kingdom: it grows
greener in winter, essence of the year;
the apple-branches musty with green fur.
In the viridian darkness of its yews

it is an enclave of perpetual vows
broken in time. Its truth shows disrepair,
disfigured shrines, their stones of gossamer,
Old Moore's astrology, all hallows,

the squire's effigy bewigged with frost,
and hobnails cracking puddles before dawn.
In grange and cottage girls rise from their beds

by candlelight and mend their ruined braids.
Touched by the cry of the iconoclast,
how the rose-window blossoms with the sun!

TWO CHORALE-PRELUDES
on melodies by Paul Celan

1. Ave Regina Coelorum

Es ist ein Land Verloren. . .

There is a land called Lost
at peace inside our heads.
The moon, full on the frost,
vivifies these stone heads.

Moods of the verb 'to stare',
split selfhoods, conjugate
ice-facets from the air,
the light glazing the light.

Look at us, Queen of Heaven!
Our solitudes drift by
your solitudes, the seven
dead stars in your sky.

2. Te Lucis Ante Terminum

Wir gehen dir, Heimat, ins Garn ...

Centaury with your staunch bloom
you there alder beech you fern,
midsummer closeness my far home,
fresh traces of lost origin.

Silvery the black cherries hang,
the plum-tree oozes through each cleft
and horse-flies siphon the green dung,
glued to the sweetness of their graft:

immortal transience, a 'kind
of otherness', self-understood,
BE FAITHFUL grows upon the mind
as lichen glimmers on the wood.

Primroses; salutations; the miry skull
of a half-eaten ram; viscous wounds in earth
opening. What seraphs are afoot.

Gold seraph to gold worm in the pierced slime:
greetings. Advent of power-in-grace. The power
of flies distracts the working of our souls.

Earth's abundance. The God–ejected Word
resorts to flesh, procures carrion, satisfies
its white hunger. Salvation's travesty

a deathless metaphor: the stale head
sauced in original blood; the little feast
foaming with cries of rapture and despair.

TERRIBILIS EST LOCUS ISTE

Gauguin and the Pont-Aven School

Briefly they are amazed. The marigold-fields
mell and shudder and the travellers,
in sudden exile burdened with remote
hieratic gestures, journey to no end

beyond the vivid severance of each day,
strangeness at doors, a different solitude
between the mirror and the window, marked
visible absences, colours of the mind,

marginal angels lightning-sketched in red
chalk on the month's accounts or marigolds
in paint runnily embossed, or the renounced
self-portrait with a seraph and a storm.

VENI CORONABERIS

A Garland for Helen Waddell

The crocus armies from the dead
rise up; the realm of love renews
the battle it was born to lose,
though for a time the snows have fled

and old stones blossom in the south
with sculpted vine and psaltery
and half-effaced adultery
the bird-dung dribbling from its mouth;

and abstinence crowns all our care
with martyr-laurels for this day.
Towers and steeples rise away
into the towering gulfs of air.

FLORENTINES

Horses, black-lidded mouths peeled back
to white: well-groomed these warriors ride,
their feuds forgotten, remembered, forgotten . . .
a cavalcade passing, night not far-off;
the stricken faces damnable and serene.

'CHRISTMAS TREES'

Bonhoeffer in his skylit cell
bleached by the flares' candescent fall,
pacing out his own citadel,

restores the broken themes of praise,
encourages our borrowed days,
by logic of his sacrifice.

Against wild reasons of the state
his words are quiet but not too quiet.
We hear too late or not too late.

TENEBRAE

He was so tired that he was scarcely
able to hear a note of the songs: he
felt imprisoned in a cold region where
his brain was numb and his spirit
was isolated.

1

Requite this angel whose
flushed and thirsting face
stoops to the sacrifice
out of which it arose.
This is the lord Eros
of grief who pities
no one; it is
Lazarus with his sores.

2

And you, who with your soft but searching voice
drew me out of the sleep where I was lost,
who held me near your heart that I might rest
confiding in the darkness of your choice:
possessed by you I chose to have no choice,
fulfilled in you I sought no further quest.
You keep me, now, in dread that quenches trust,
in desolation where my sins rejoice.
As I am passionate so you with pain
turn my desire; as you seem passionless
so I recoil from all that I would gain,
wounding myself upon forgetfulness,
false ecstasies, which you in truth sustain
as you sustain each item of your cross.

3

Veni Redemptor, but not in our time.
Christus Resurgens, quite out of this world.
'Ave' we cry; the echoes are returned.
Amor Carnalis is our dwelling-place.

4

O light of light, supreme delight;
grace on our lips to our disgrace.
Time roosts on all such golden wrists;
our leanness is our luxury.
Our love is what we love to have;
our faith is in our festivals.

5

Stupefying images of grief-in-dream,
succubae to my natural grief of heart,
cling to me, then; you who will not desert
your love nor lose him in some blank of time.
You come with all the licence of her name
to tell me you are mine. But you are not
and she is not. Can my own breath be hurt
by breathless shadows groaning in their game?
It can. The best societies of hell
acknowledge this, aroused by what they know:
consummate rage recaptured there in full
as faithfulness demands it, blow for blow,
and rectitude that mimics its own fall
reeling with sensual abstinence and woe.

6

This is the ash-pit of the lily-fire,
this is the questioning at the long tables,
this is true marriage of the self-in-self,
this is a raging solitude of desire,
this is the chorus of obscene consent,
this is a single voice of purest praise.

7

He wounds with ecstasy. All
the wounds are his own.
He wears the martyr's crown.
He is the Lord of Misrule.
He is the Master of the Leaping Figures,
the motley factions.
Revelling in auguries
he is the Weeper of the Valedictions.

8

Music survives, composing her own sphere,
Angel of Tones, Medusa, Queen of the Air,
and when we would accost her with real cries
silver on silver thrills itself to ice.

ACKNOWLEDGMENTS

THE PENTECOST CASTLE: parts of this sequence originally appeared in *Agenda* Vol. 10 no. 4 – Vol. 11 no. 1; Vol. 11 no. 4 – Vol. 12 no. 1; Vol. 13 no. 3.

LACHRIMAE was first published in *Agenda* Vol. 12 no. 4 – Vol. 13 no. 1 and was reprinted in the P.E.N. anthology *New Poems 1975* (Hutchinson).

AN APOLOGY FOR THE REVIVAL OF CHRISTIAN ARCHITECTURE IN ENGLAND: Three sonnets (nos. 3, 8, 12) first appeared with this title in John Heath-Stubbs and Martin Green, ed., *Homage to George Barker on his Sixtieth Birthday* (Martin Brian and O'Keeffe, 1973). With the title 'On the Death of Mr Shakespeare' the first, seventh and eleventh sonnets were a response to a commission from the World Centre for Shakespeare Studies Ltd, and were read at the Bankside Globe Playhouse, London, on April 23rd 1976 as part of the programme 'Poems for Shakespeare'. Together with the fourth, fifth, ninth and thirteenth sonnets they were first printed in *Agenda* Vol. 15 nos. 2–3. The second sonnet first appeared in the privately-printed *Hand and Eye: an Anthology for Sacheverell Sitwell*, 1977, edited by Geoffrey Elborn. The tenth sonnet was first published in *Poetry Nation 3*.

TENEBRAE: The fourth, sixth and eighth sections (together with 'Christmas Trees') originally formed part of a cantata-text, *Ad Incensum Lucernae,* set to music by James Brown and first performed in Emmanuel Church, Leeds, on February 5th 1975. The sequence was published in the Paris Review #75.

Other poems first appeared in *Agenda, Poetry Nation, Shenandoah, Stand,* and *Harvard Magazine.*

Spanish and German poems have provided points of departure for several poems in this book. 'The Pentecost Castle' is particularly indebted to J. M. Cohen's *Penguin Book of Spanish Verse*. The final sonnet of 'Lachrimae' is a free translation of a sonnet by Lope de Vega (Cohen, p. 247) and the second sonnet of 'An Apology . . .' is an imitation of a sonnet by L. L. de Argensola (Cohen, p. 202). The poems by Paul Celan on which I have based my 'Two Chorale-Preludes' are from *Die Niemandsrose* (1963).

*

'A Pre-Raphaelite Notebook' adapts a sentence from Pascal's *Pensées*. The last line of 'Quaint Mazes' is indebted to Ronald Blythe, 'Satan without Seraphs' in *The Listener*, February 4th 1971. 'Te Lucis Ante Terminum' quotes a phrase from Walter J. Ong SJ, 'Voice as Summons for Belief' (*Literature and Belief: English Institute Essays* (1957) 1958, p. 84).

*

The epigraph for this book is taken from *The Collected Poems of Sidney Keyes* (1945). I am grateful to Routledge and Kegan Paul Ltd for permission to quote. I also gratefully acknowledge the permission of Oxford University Press for the quotations from Imogen Holst, *The Music of Gustav Holst* (second edition 1968), and Simone Weil, *First and Last Notebooks* translated by Richard Rees, 1970; and of Macmillan Publishing Co., Inc., for the quotation from *The Letters of W. B. Yeats,* ed. Allan Wade (copyright 1953, 1954 by Anne Butler Yeats).